Playing It Right!

Social Skills Activities for Parents and Teachers of Young Children with Autism Spectrum Disorders, Including Asperger Syndrome and Autism

Playing It Right!

**Social Skills Activities for Parents and Teachers of
Young Children with Autism Spectrum Disorders,
Including Asperger Syndrome and Autism**

Rachael Bareket

Autism Asperger Publishing Co.
P.O. Box 23173
Shawnee Mission, Kansas 66283-0173
www.asperger.net

©2006 Autism Asperger Publishing Company
P.O. Box 23173
Shawnee Mission, KS 66283-0173
www.asperger.net

Publisher's Cataloging-in-Publication

Bareket, Rachael.
    Playing it right! : social skills activities for parents and teachers of young children with autism spectrum disorders, including Asperger syndrome and autism / Rachael Bareket. – 1st ed. – Shawnee Mission, Kan. : Autism Asperger Publishing, 2006.

        p. ; cm.

        ISBN-13: 978-1-931282-81-9
        ISBN-10: 1-931282-81-1
        LCCN: 2005935988
        Presents a series of games and activities that parents and teachers can use to develop and enhance the social skills of young children with autism spectrum disorders.
        Includes bibliographical references.

        1. Autistic children–Behavior modification. 2. Autistic children–Behavior modification–Programmed instruction. 3. Social skills in children–Study and teaching. 4. Autism in children. 5. Asperger's syndrome. 6. Autistic children–Education. I. Title.

RJ506.A9 B37 2006   2005935988
618.92/85882--dc22   0601

This book is designed in Benguiat Frisky and Helvetica Neue.

Printed in the United States of America

Acknowledgments

Many wonderful people have contributed to this book. My thanks to the fantastic teachers and aides who implement some of the strategies, Debbie McCallum, Sarah Buchner, Debbie Myerson, Angela Monihan, and Aliza Deutsch. My sincere thanks also to Catherine Booth, Daphne Gadde, and Rae Silverstein for their support. Thanks to my proofreaders, Debbie Myerson and Michelle Aaronson, and a special thank-you to Gayle Ward for her insight and excellent contributions. Thank you also to Simone Zmood, Anthony Goldberg, and Jacob Stzokman for technical support.

Last and not least, I thank my husband, Chezi, for believing I could do this, and my son, for his contribution to this book and his ability to succeed in the face of adversity while filling our hearts with joy.

– R. Bareket

Table of Contents

Introduction

Like all children, every child on the autism spectrum has a unique personality and combination of characteristics. Some children who are mildly affected may show only slight delays in language and face greater challenges with social interactions. The social world is very complex, and children with a developmental delay in this area need basic tools to help them succeed in their friendships and to communicate effectively in the world. For example, they may have difficulty initiating and/or maintaining a conversation, have problems recognizing their own and others' emotions, their communication is often described as talking at others instead of to them, they have difficulty controlling their emotions when frustrated, and so on. Socializing is so much more than verbal communication. It's about nonverbal cues like facial expressions, how to control one's anger, learning to wait and not invading another person's space, and similar behaviors that are crucial in everyday interactions with others.

While a speech-language therapist can concentrate on working with the child on verbal communication, a special program to address a child's social interaction is important to help develop effective social skills. Particularly because children with autism spectrum disorders do not pick up cues from their environment, as do most of their neurotypical peers, they need direct, specific instruction. Often such training is not offered in schools.

How to Use This Book

Playing It Right! is a series of activities designed to help children on the autism spectrum develop basic social skills by focusing on elements of social interaction in a variety of settings – home, preschool, kindergarten, and elementary school. The book is intended for use by parents, teachers, and others working with young children of varying ages, depending on their level of social skills and where they fall on the autism spectrum. The activities may be carried out either one-on-one with the child or in groups such as in preschool, kindergarten or early elementary classes. Individual activities may be chosen to address a specific social skill, or the whole series of activities may be built into the curriculum or social skills program.

The posters that result from many of the activities may be hung on the classroom wall or the home refrigerator to serve as a visual reminder to the child. If you are able to photocopy and enlarge the posters, this will give you more room to work with and make it easier for the children to handle. Also, laminating finished work and cards is recommended as the materials will hold up better and last longer.

Not every child will be able to concentrate long enough to complete a whole activity in one session. Posters can be an ongoing project, and the various games can be played several times over. It is important to make sure that games and activities are fun for the children. To motivate the child to become engaged and maintain his or her interest, it is helpful to have rewards and incentives on hand. This can be anything the child enjoys; the possibilities are endless, and include blowing bubbles, jumping on a trampoline, and getting stickers from the child's area of interest (for example, trains, lizards, horses). In addition, samples of specially designed reward cards may be found in the Appendix, pages 56-58.

Once the posters and cards have served their primary goal as visual aids, they may be included in a scrapbook as a record of the child's work and social skills achievements. The scrapbook can be shared at school with other professionals working with the child, or at home with parents and other family members as a proud record of the child's accomplishments. In addition, it may be used if certain behaviors need to be modified. You can then use the book to remind the child of the appropriate social behavior. Finally, having a copy of the book both at home and at school gives the child the opportunity to apply new skills in a variety of situations – an important step in generalization.

To carry out the activities, you will need commonly available items such as pens/pencils, scissors, glue, etc., as listed under each activity, in addition to the specific models and templates provided in the Appendix. Whenever you individualize materials to suit the needs of a particular child, you may use freehand drawings or such software packages as Boardmaker (www.mayer-johnson.com) and Kidspiration® Software (Inspiration Software®, Inc.; www.strategictransitions.com) to support or replace the text with visuals. Due to their unique learning style, visuals are important for many learners on the autism spectrum as well as for non-readers.

Visual Schedules and Choice Boards

Due to their need for structure and predictability, most children on the autism spectrum find it helpful to have a visual concept of what their day, week, or even vacation will be like. In addition to ensuring that the day runs smoothly, the predictability of schedules and other visual supports can help prevent emotional outbursts and meltdowns by relieving anxiety associated with not knowing what is "going to happen next." While not directly part of a social skills program, several examples of visual schedules have been included in the Appendix on pages 60-64.

Choosing an Activity

Focusing on some of the major challenges children on the autism spectrum face in the social realm, *Playing It Right!* offers the following structured activities: Relationships, Learning to Listen, My Special Space, Waiting, Learning About Emotions, Dealing With Anger, Speaking Politely, Using Our Voices: Learning to Speak More Quietly and With the Appropriate Emotion, Cooperation, and Friendship.

The following checklist will help you identify which of the child's social skills are lacking and the best activity to help develop and work on those skills.

Social Skills Checklist

Social Issue The child:	Yes (X)	Section	Page
Has limited concept of family relationships		**Relationships**	4
Has poor eye contact		**Learning to Listen**	6, 7
Is unable to stay still while listening		**Learning to Listen**	8
Fails to reply when spoken to		**Learning to Listen**	8
Tends to invade others' body space		**My Special Space**	11
Squeezes/hugs too tightly		**My Special Space**	11
Finds it difficult to discern when and with whom to share body space		**My Special Space**	12
Has difficulty waiting		**Waiting**	15
Is unable to read others' emotion		**Learning About Emotions**	19
Demonstrates anger out of proportion to a given situation		**Dealing With Anger**	28
Is unable to control anger		**Dealing With Anger**	31
Uses impolite and inappropriate language		**Speaking Politely**	34
Uses inappropriately loud voice with no control of dynamics		**Using Our Voices**	36
Is unable to discern emotion in voice		**Using Our Voices**	40
Uses wrong emotion in voice		**Using Our Voices**	40
Demonstrates oppositional behavior (no cooperation)		**Cooperation**	41
Is unable to understand the perspective of others		**Cooperation/Friendship**	41, 46-50
Has difficulty understanding the dynamics of play		**Friendship**	46
Has difficulty discerning who friends are		**Friendship**	45, 50
Becomes anxious from not knowing "what will happen next" or during unstructured times		**Schedules to Relieve Anxiety**	59

Relationships

A family tree poster is a great way for a child to learn about relationships. Make the poster with the child and hang it on the refrigerator or classroom wall. Discuss it with the child. At home, explain family relationships before seeing or phoning family members.

For example,
- "Aunty Jo is coming over tonight. She is my sister."
- "We are going to Nana's house. She is your grandmother and you are her grandson. Nana is my mommy and you are my son."

Activity: My Family Tree

✔ **Materials**
- photos of family members
- scissors
- glue
- copies of pages 69-70

NOTE: Here and throughout the activities, please make sufficient copies based on the number of children in your group.

✔ Cut out pictures of family members and glue them to the tree. Write their names underneath the corresponding photos. (This also helps the child learn to read and write.) Glue a label (see below) under the name to explain a given person's relationship to the child.

grandparent	grandparent	grandparent	grandparent	grandparent
aunt	aunt	aunt	aunt	aunt
uncle	uncle	uncle	uncle	uncle
brother	brother	brother	brother	brother
sister	sister	sister	sister	sister
cousin	cousin	cousin	cousin	cousin

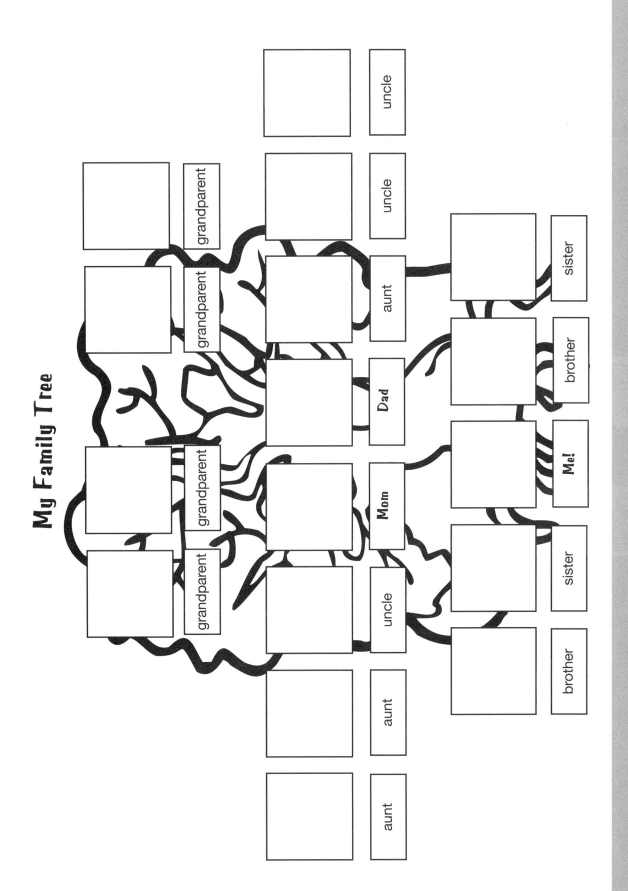

My Family Tree

grandparent

grandparent

grandparent

grandparent

uncle

uncle

aunt

Dad

Mom

uncle

aunt

aunt

sister

brother

Me!

sister

brother

Learning to Listen

Adapted from *Socially Speaking* (Shroeder, 1996).
Used with permission.

When you speak to a child, she may hear what you
are saying but not show the typical signs of listening.
That is, she may not be making eye contact; may fidget
and not reply; or talk while being addressed.

There are several steps to follow when learning to become a good
listener. Here we will explore: Look at the Person, Don't Bump Words,
Keep Still, and Reply.

Step One: Look at the Person (Eye Contact)

Activity One: Draw Your Eyes

✔ **Materials**

- small mirror
- colored markers
- glue
- copies of page 71

Using a mirror, ask the child to draw her eyes in the box on page 71. Hold a
discussion around the importance of using one's eyes, in general, and to show
attention and interest, in particular.

I look at the person I'm listening to with my eyes:

Activity Two: Winking Game

Practice making eye contact by taking turns winking. In school, the "wink" can be passed around in a circle. This activity can be part of a game where the children follow the adult's directions to clap, nod, stomp their feet, etc.

Activity Three: Find My Eyes

Play a version of "hide and go seek" where the child has to make eye contact with you when you find her. This activity is best played one-on-one to begin with but may be extended to several children when the rules are understood and practiced.

Step Two: Don't Bump Words

Activity One: Don't Interrupt

While the child is talking to you, interrupt him and then explain that you are "bumping words" with each other. Explain what happens when you interrupt – the other person feels ignored, gets mad, etc. Practice talking to each other without "bumping words."

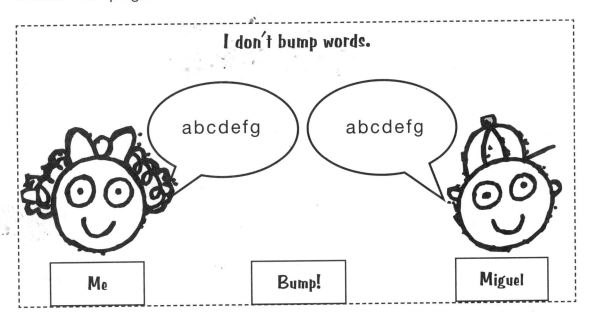

In the box on page 71, ask the child to draw himself and another person bumping words. (Add the person's name in the right-hand, lower rectangle. This personalizes the activity and makes it more meaningful for the child.)

Step Three: Keep Still

Ask the child to draw a picture of himself standing still in the box on page 71.

Activity: Statues

Play a game of "statues." In this version of this popular game, everyone has to stand still and make eye contact with someone when somebody calls out "statue." Have children take turns calling out "statue."

Step Four: Reply

Practice replying with the good listening poster (see page 10).

Activity One: "I Went to the Zoo"

In preparation for the game, face the child and remind her to make eye contact ("show me your eyes") and keep still. The first person says, "I went to the zoo and I saw a zebra." The next person repeats this statement and adds new information. For example: "I went to the zoo and I saw a zebra and an elephant ...," etc. (This may be played one-on-one, but is best played with a group of children sitting in a circle. If you are playing the game in a group, make sure each child turns to the person he or she is talking to in the circle and obeys the listening rules.) In addition to the emphasis on making a reply when being addressed, this activity teaches children to pay attention and remember what was said.

Activity Two: Model Good Listening

Model good listening by asking the child/children to determine whether you are listening to them or not. Ask the question, and when the child answers, either look away, fidget, and talk to yourself (*not listening)* or look straight at the child, keep still, and do not interrupt (*listening*).

As a group activity, practicing good and bad listening can be lots of fun. Children can pair up and show good and bad listening to the rest of the class. The activity may also be done in a school drama class as the children can demonstrate good and bad listening on stage for the rest of the group. *Regardless of how you do it, be sure that it is clear to the children when they are using good listening and the negative consequences of "bad" listening.*

Review the completed "Good Listening" poster. Explain that these are the rules for good listening.

Poster – Good Listening

1. Look at the Person

2. Don't Bump Words

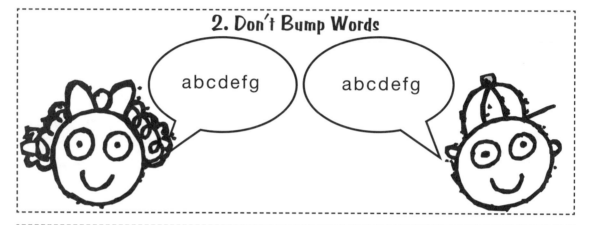

abcdefg   abcdefg

3. Keep Still

4. Reply

My Special Space

Invading someone's space includes standing too close, squeezing somebody or even hugging a person too tightly. This is often an area of difficulty for children with autism spectrum disorders. The following activities help children to understand about personal space by showing that we all have a "special space" around our bodies that must be obeyed.

Activity One: My Special Space
✔ Materials
- a piece of newsprint/butcher paper larger than the child
- different-colored crayons

Place the paper on the floor and ask the child to lie down on it. Draw her outline. Then draw a space around the child's body in a different color to show her "special space." Color in the space together while discussing the concept of personal space. This activity may also be done in a class where all the children make an outline of themselves and draw in their "special space."

Activity Two: This Is My Space
✔ Materials
- hula-hoops

Hold a hula-hoop around yourself to show your special space. If the child is persistently invading your space, try sitting with the hoop around you and making a rule that the child can only enter your space for hugs. Using the hula-hoops, have the children try to get a feeling for how much space they need to feel comfortable and to understand that they must respect and honor other children's space.

✔ A Squeeze Is Not a Hug!!
If the child is hugging too hard or squeezing others' arms, provide a squeezable or stretchy rubber toy (can be kept in the child's pocket). Ask the child to squeeze the toy every time he wants to squeeze somebody.

Activity Three: Poster – How Close Can I Get?

Make a poster showing when the child can share his space and when he cannot.

✔ **Materials**
- coloring pens, pencils or crayons
- old magazines
- family photos showing people hugging
- glue
- scissors
- your own drawings (stick figures are O.K.)
- copies of pages 72-73

Who Can I Share My Space With?

With Family, and Sometimes With Teachers and Friends:

Not When We Are Playing or Working:

Never With Strangers:

13

Pictures and Labels to Cut out and Glue on the Poster

Family	Friends or Teachers	Strangers
I hug my family!	We don't share our space with friends when they are busy!	
I love to hug my sister.	Sometimes we share our space with friends.	
	Sometimes I need to hug my teacher. (preschool)	
	We don't share space when we are busy in class.	
	I don't share my space during line-up.	

✔ Next time you are walking in the street, show the child that strangers keep a space between them. Videos and movies are also excellent teaching tools.

Waiting

Waiting is very difficult for some children. The following two exercises help the child to learn when to wait and how to wait.

Activity One: Poster – When Do I Need to Wait?

Make a poster of times when a child might need to wait. This activity can be done at school or at home.

✔ Materials
- coloring pens/pencils
- old magazines
- a photo of the child (passport size)
- glue
- scissors
- your own drawings (stick figures are O.K.)
- copies of materials on pages 74-76

When Do I Need to Wait?

Picture of Child

Picture of Me Waiting When ...

I want to swing.

Pictures and Labels to Cut out and Glue on the Poster
I Need to Wait When ...

Someone is on the phone.	People are talking.	Dad's cooking.	Mom's feeding the baby.
Mom's bathing the baby.	The teacher is busy.	Someone's watching TV.	My friends are in the middle of playing a game.

Activity Two: What Should I Do While I'm Waiting?

As a visual reminder, make a card for the child to keep in her pocket or backpack to remind her of how to wait – that is, what she can do to occupy herself appropriately.

Pictures and Labels to Cut out and Glue on the "Wait Card"

Say "Excuse Me."

Take a deep breath.

Count to 10.

12345678910

Don't bump words.

Stay out of people's space.

Go and play.

Go and play.

Use my squeezable.

✔ Laminating the card will make it more sturdy and last longer.

Learning About Emotions

Children with autism spectrum disorders have difficulty understanding their own as well as reading the emotions of others. Nonverbal behavior plays an important part in all social interactions, putting these children at a distinct disadvantage when playing and communicating with others.

✔ **Materials**
- mirrors
- scissors
- colored pens and pencils
- poster board
- glue
- pictures or photos showing different emotions
- copies of pages 77-85

Step One: Reading Emotions

Activity One: Identifying Emotions

On the following table, ask the child to point to or circle a facial expression to match the emotion. Discuss why he chose a particular expression.

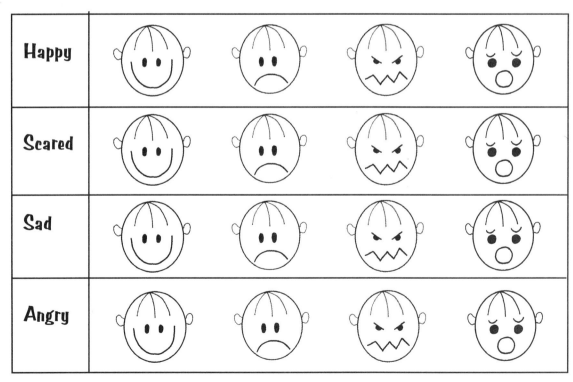

Happy				
Scared				
Sad				
Angry				

Graphics by D. McCallum

Activity Two: Emotions "Snap" and "Memory"

✔ Cut out the pictures on pages 78-79 to make a set of "snap" cards. (Laminating the pages before cutting will make them last longer.) Use the cards to play "Emotions Snap" and "Memory."

Happy	Happy	Sad
Happy	Sad	Sad
Happy	Sad	Angry
Angry	Scared	Scared

Concepts and graphics by D. McCallum

Step Two: Practice Emotions

Activity One: Practice in the Mirror

Cut out the following happy, sad, frustrated, and angry faces and glue them next to a mirror. Have the child practice making the different faces. In doing so, discuss what to look for and try to replicate.

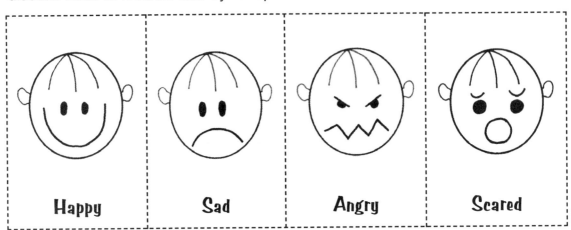

| Happy | Sad | Angry | Scared |

Graphics by D. McCallum

✔ Alternatively, take photos of a family member or classmate showing the emotions and put them around the mirror. Repeat as above.

Activity Two: Guess How I'm Feeling

Sit opposite the child and show her different expressions. Ask her to guess which emotion you are expressing and discuss how she decides.

Activity Three: Posters – Emotions

Concept: D. McCallum

Take photos of classmates or friends showing different emotions. Make posters of each emotion and hang them on the wall. For example: a happy poster, sad poster, proud poster, etc. As children demonstrate the various emotions during the day, have them point to the poster to reinforce the idea.

Step Three: Reading Social Situations

Activity: Spot the Emotion

In each of the following drawings, ask the child: "How is the child feeling?" (happy, sad, sacred or angry) and have him circle the correct emotion. Then ask, "Why does the child feel this way?" You can write the response in the "Why" section if the child is unable to do so himself.

 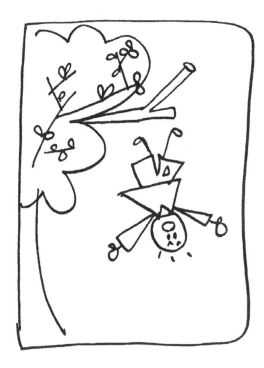

The child feels (circle):

Happy   Sad   Angry   Scared   Happy   Sad   Angry   Scared

Why? _____   Why? _____

_____   _____

The child feels (circle):

Happy   Sad   Angry   Scared   Happy   Sad   Angry   Scared

Why? _____   Why? _____

_____   _____

The child feels (circle):

Happy　　Sad　　Angry　　Scared

Why? _____

_____

Happy　　Sad　　Angry　　Scared

Why? _____

_____

The child feels (circle):

Happy   Sad   Angry   Scared   Happy   Sad   Angry   Scared

Why? _____   Why? _____

_____   _____

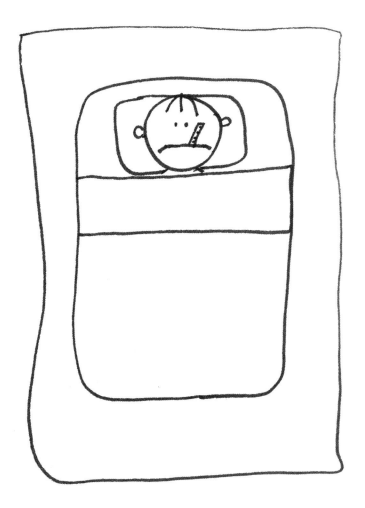

The child feels (circle):

Happy   Sad   Angry   Scared

Why? _____

_____   _____

Dealing With Anger

Many children with autism spectrum disorders have trouble understanding and controlling their emotions. As a result, often their anger level appears to be out of proportion to a given situation.

The following activities show children that there are different levels of anger and that it is possible to regulate one's emotions and, therefore, avoid or reduce the occurrence of "meltdowns."

Activity One: The Grouchometer

Adapted from *Navigating the Social World* (McAfee, 2002). Used with permission.

✔**Materials**
- pens/pencils
- copies of pages 86-88

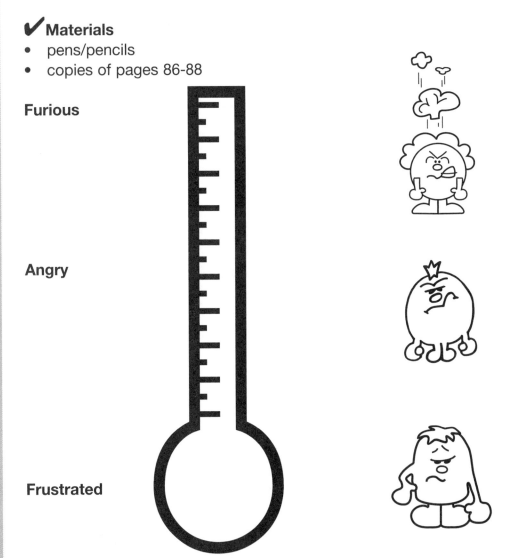

Furious

Angry

Frustrated

Use the Grouchometer to help the child visually measure her feelings of anger. Talk about the situation and get the child to decide how angry she would be in the potential situation. Then have her circle the correct anger level and shade in the corresponding area.

How Angry Am I?	Draw a Circle Around the Matching Level of Anger		
Putting together a difficult puzzle	Frustrated	Angry	Furious
Waiting	Frustrated	Angry	Furious
Losing my favorite toy	Frustrated	Angry	Furious

How Angry Am I?	Draw a Circle Around the Matching Level of Anger
Falling over	**Frustrated** **Angry** **Furious**
Someone hits me	**Frustrated** **Angry** **Furious**
Computer problem	**Frustrated** **Angry** **Furious**

Activity Two: What Should I Do When I'm Angry?

Once the child begins to understand that there are several levels of anger and that they can be modulated/regulated, teach him options for dealing with anger. As part of this process, make a card for the child to keep in his pocket or backpack to remind him of how to calm down.

Pictures and Labels to Cut out and Glue on the Child's "Anger Card"

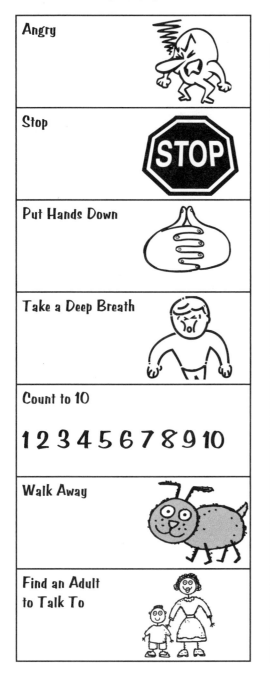

Anger Card

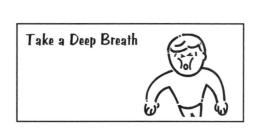

✔ Laminating the card will make it last longer.

✔ Put favorite stickers on the other side of the card to help the child to distract himself from being angry and help him feel better.

Activity Three: "Happy Book"

Adapted from *Navigating the Social World* (McAfee, 2002). Used with permission.

✔**Materials**
- coloring pens and pencils
- a scrapbook
- photos of happy events (happy faces) from old magazines or family photos
- stickers or pictures of interests from old magazines or family photos (e.g., trains, lizards, horses)
- glue
- scissors

Using the above materials, make a "Happy Book" for a child to look at when he is feeling sad or angry. This is a great activity to do together as you can discuss the various feelings along the way. Decorate the cover with happy photos and dedicate pages to the child's special interests and favorite things to do (e.g., a train page).

Activity Four: Activity Box (age 5+)

✔**Materials**
- empty tissue box
- copies of page 90
- scissors
- items for decorating the box, including glue to affix them with

Decorate the box and fill it with calming activity cards for the child to use when feeling angry or frustrated. The child chooses a card and completes the task designated before either choosing another card or returning to the class if adequately calm. Some of these activities need the supervision of an adult (e.g., going for a walk). As always, the proposed activities may be individualized to make sure they are appropriate and enjoyable to a given child.

Calming Activity Cards

Play on the computer.	Draw a picture about how you are feeling.
Play a quiet game such as a puzzle.	Go for a walk.
Go for a run.	Take a rest.
Write a story about how you are feeling.	Listen to a story tape.
Play with your stress ball.	Visit another teacher or friend.

Concept: Pam Langford and Debbie McCallum

✔ Laminating the cards will make them more durable.

✔ It is helpful for parents and teachers to learn to recognize early warning signs of anger to prevent meltdowns. This allows you to direct the child to look at his Anger Card, "Happy Book," or activity box and possibly prevent a full-scale outburst.

Speaking Politely

Many children need help in expressing themselves in a polite way. The "Trash Program" is a helpful way of giving them polite alternatives, and helping them to understand that the way they express themselves affects people's emotions and attitudes toward them.

Activity: The Trash Program

✔ **Materials**
- black marker
- red marker
- copies of page 91

Using the table on page 91, write or draw something (in black) in the Not Nice! column that the child has said that is impolite or unkind. The pictures in the next column show the child how this might make someone feel sad, angry, etc. Draw a red cross over the words and tell the child that you are "feeding the words to the trash monster" and making them go away. Then help the child think of a nicer way of saying the impolite/unkind comment and write it in the "Better" column. Talk about how it would make someone happier to hear these words instead (see last column).

Not Nice!		**Feed It to the Trash Monster!**		**Better!**

I hate you!

I am upset with you.

Using Our Voices: Learning to Speak More Quietly and With the Appropriate Emotion

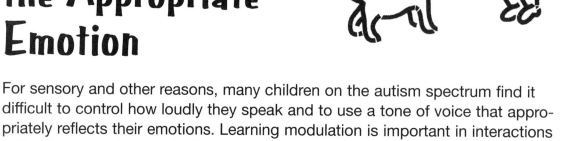

For sensory and other reasons, many children on the autism spectrum find it difficult to control how loudly they speak and to use a tone of voice that appropriately reflects their emotions. Learning modulation is important in interactions with others as it is part of effective communication.

For example:
- Eddie uses an angry tone of voice when he says "Help me with this puzzle."
- Even when close by, John speaks so loudly that the other children cover their ears and move away.

Music is a fun and effective way to help children understand and control their voice tone and volume. Parents can do these activities with their child at home, or they can be done as a group activity at school.

Step One: Dynamics

Activity One: Soft, Medium, and Loud Voices

Using an instrument can make it easier to demonstrate "soft," "medium" and "loud" sounds. Ask the child to copy you. Keep practicing.

✔ **Materials**
- musical instruments of your choice (piano, recorder, drum, etc.)
- copies of page 92

✔ Remember, it doesn't need to sound melodic.

Activity Two: Practice Using Your Voice

Say :

"soft voice" (softly)

"medium voice" (moderately)

"loud voice" (loudly)

Get the child to copy you and keep practicing.

✔ A soft voice is not a whisper; learning to whisper needs practice too!

✔ If the child is speaking too loudly, say "use your soft voice" or "use your medium voice" and talk to him the way he should be speaking, depending on the situation.

For example:
Miguel (loud voice): "I want another sandwich."
Mom: "Use your medium voice. I'm right here; I hear you. OK, I'll make you a sandwich."
Mom says this in a medium voice.

Activity Three: Which Voice Do I Use?

Use this activity to help the child figure out which voice to use. Ask the child to circle which voice she would use in the following locations. Discuss with the child which variables to consider when deciding on which voice to be used.

✔ **Materials**
- pens/pencils
- copies of pages 93-94

Which Voice Do I Use?

Place	Voice		
In the park	Soft Voice	Medium Voice	Loud Voice
At the library	Soft Voice	Medium Voice	Loud Voice
In the classroom	Soft Voice	Medium Voice	Loud Voice
At home	Soft Voice	Medium Voice	Loud Voice
At the zoo	Soft Voice	Medium Voice	Loud Voice
In a shop	Soft Voice	Medium Voice	Loud Voice

Which Voice Do I Use? (cont.)

Place	Voice		
In the street	Soft Voice	Medium Voice	Loud Voice
At the mall	Soft Voice	Medium Voice	Loud Voice
At someone's house	Soft Voice	Medium Voice	Loud Voice
In a hospital	Soft Voice	Medium Voice	Loud Voice
At the movies	Soft Voice	Medium Voice	Loud Voice
In the car	Soft Voice	Medium Voice	Loud Voice
On a bus or train	Soft Voice	Medium Voice	Loud Voice

Step Two: Learning About Voice Tone

Activity One: What Type of Voice?

✔ Materials
- Kids' TV programs or videos (videos or DVDs are particularly helpful because you can rewind and play them again). When watching children's shows, point out to the child what type of voice the various characters are using and in which situations.
- Happy voice
- Angry voice
- Sad voice
- Frustrated voice

Ask the child to tell you which voice a given character is using. You can also hold a competition with the child to see who can identify the voice first (happy, sad, angry or frustrated).

Activity Two: Let's Practice!

Practice using happy, sad, angry or frustrated voices by using sentences such as the following:
- I'm happy because I just got an ice cream cone.
- I'm angry because I broke my new toy train.
- I'm sad because my grandma went away.
- I'm frustrated because I can't build my Lego car.

✔ If you hear the child using an inappropriate tone of voice, stop and point it out to her. Then briefly explore what would have been the correct tone, given the situation.

For example:
Hairdresser:　　　　　"Tim, you've been really good, would you like a lollipop?"
Tim (angry voice):　"I don't want a lollipop!"
Mom (happy voice)　"Use your happy voice, Tim. 'I don't want a lollipop thank you.'"

✔ Remember, it is also important to point out when a child is using a correct tone of voice.

Cooperation

Part of socializing and learning effective social skills is to recognize that people do things for each other; there's an often unconscious give-and-take. This requires more than simply teaching a child to listen. Just because the child listens, does not mean that she will do what you ask of her, as illustrated in the following example:

"Monica, I need you to listen. Please finish your art project." Monica listens and then returns to watching television without as much as looking in the direction of the project.

The following activity can be done at school or at home.

Activity One: Poster – "Listen and Do"

✔ **Materials**
- colored pens/pencils
- old magazines
- photo of the child
- glue
- scissors
- your own drawings (stick figures are O.K.)
- copies of pages 95-97

Make a "Listen and Do" poster using pictures (cut out from old magazines, draw or cut out and paste those on page 97) to illustrate all the things that we do for each other. The focus should be on the typical and necessary requests you make of the child at home or at school, such as "go to bed" or "go sit on the mat with the other children." Use words with the pictures to help with reading skills.

This activity may be completed in one session or as an ongoing project. Hang the poster on the refrigerator or classroom wall and add new ideas as appropriate.

Mom and Dad Do Things for Me ...

Photo of
child

So I Will Listen AND Do Things for Them.

My Teachers Do Things for Me ...

Photo of child

So I Will Listen AND Do Things for Them.

Pictures and Labels to Cut out and Glue on the Poster

Things Mom and Dad Do for Me	Things I Can Do for Mom and Dad	Things My Teachers Do for Me	Things I Can Do for My Teachers
Play with me	Brush my teeth when asked to	Hug me when I'm sad (Preschool)	Sit on the mat and listen
Read to me	Go to bed	Help me with painting and drawing	Use my quiet voice inside
Take me to the zoo	Get in the bath or shower when asked to	Teach me games	Eat lunch when asked to
Take me to the beach	Eat breakfast when served	Read to me	Do my work
Make yummy food	Get dressed when it's time	Take me on a field trip	Line up quietly
Give me hugs and kisses	Feed the dog	Help me finish my work	Be good to other kids

✔ It is helpful to include the child's special interest on the poster. This will ensure you have his attention. For example: Dad takes me to see trains.

Friendship

Due to their difficulties in the area of turn taking, theory of mind (taking another person's perspective), as well as general communication challenges, many children with autism spectrum disorders have problems making and keeping friends. The following two activities help children understand that friendship is a two-way street.

Activity One: Who Are My Friends?

✔ **Materials**
- pencils, colored pens

Draw a picture of your friends:

What are my friends' names? (You can write these for the child if she is unable to do so.) _____

Activity Two: Poster – Friends Do Things for Each Other

✔ **Materials**

- colored pens/pencils
- old magazines
- photo of the child
- glue
- scissors
- your own drawings (stick figures are O.K.)
- copies of pages 98-100

Make the "Friends" poster on page 47 to illustrate all the things that friends do for each other. This exercise can be done at home, and is also ideal for a school group. Once again, use words with the pictures to help with general understanding as well as reading skills.

✔ A good time to practice these skills is when children are playing with each other. Remind them to take turns and listen to each other.

For example:
"Ben, I think it's Aaron's turn to choose a game."
"Aaron has a good idea; stop and listen to him."

Things My Friends Do for Me

Things I Can Do for My Friends

Photo of child

Pictures and Labels to Cut out and Glue on the Poster

Things My Friends Do for Me	Things I Can Do for My Friends
Listen to me	Listen to them
Talk about what I like	Talk about what they like
Play what I like	Play what they like
Teach me games	Use my happy voice
Take turns	Take turns

Pictures and Labels to Cut out and Glue on the Poster (cont.)

Things My Friends Do for Me	Things I Can Do for My Friends
Not bump words with me	Don't bump words with them
Use a medium voice, not a loud voice	Use a medium voice, not a loud voice
Stay out of my space	Stay out of their space
Help me when I am stuck	Help them when they are stuck
Be happy when I win	Be happy when they win
Don't tease me	Don't tease them

Activity Three: Who Are My Good Friends? (age 5+)
Activity by Gayle Ward

✔ Materials
- pens/pencils
- copies of page 101

Ask the child to list her friends (you might need to help write the names down). Using the "Friends" poster (see page 47) as a guide as well as the child's own suggestions, ask the child what he likes about his friends. Examples may include "they don't tease me," "they help me when I am stuck," "they talk nicely to me," etc. Using the child's criteria, go back over the list of names to help determine who her good friends are, and who might not be her friend. If appropriate, try to intersperse something into the conversation about bullies – how to spot them, what to do if you are being bullied, etc.

My Friends	What I Like About Them
Susie	She eats lunch with me.
Jody	Talks to me in class.
Tyler	Plays at recess with me.
Carley	Helps me with my school-work.

References

Gray, C. (2000). *Comic book conversations. Colorful interactions with students with autism and related disorders.* Jenison, MI: Jenison Public Schools.

Gutstein, S. E., & Sheely, R. K. (2002). *Relationship development intervention with young children. Social and emotional development activities for Asperger's Syndrome, autism, PDD and NLD.* London: Jessica Kingsley Publishers Ltd.

Howlin, P., Baron Cohen, S., & Hadwin, J. (1999). *Teaching children with autism to mind-read. A practical guide.* Chichester, UK: John Wiley.

McAfee, J. (2002). *Navigating the social world. A curriculum for individuals with Asperger's Syndrome, high functioning autism and related disorders.* Ft. Worth, TX: Future Horizons Inc.

Santomauro, J. (1999). *Set for gold. Strategies for life.* Brisbane, Australia: Author.

Schroeder, A. (1996). *Socially speaking. A pragmatic social skills programme for primary students.* Cambridge, UK: LDA.

Further Reading

Attwood, T. (1997). *Asperger's Syndrome. A guide for parents and professionals.* London: Jessica Kingsley Publishers Ltd.

Baker, J. (2001). *The social skills picture book. Teaching play, emotion, and communication to children with autism.* Ft. Worth, TX: Future Horizons Inc.

Baker, J. (2003). *Social skills training for children and adolescents with Asperger Syndrome and social-communication problems.* Shawnee Mission, KS: Autism Asperger Publishing Company.

Buron, K. D. (2003). *When my autism gets too big! A relaxation book for children with autism spectrum disorders.* Shawnee Mission, KS: Autism Asperger Publishing Company.

Buron, K. D., & Curtis, M. (2002). *The incredible 5-point scale.* Shawnee Mission, KS: Autism Asperger Publishing Company.

Cardon, T. A. (2004). *Let's talk emotions: Helping children with social cognitive deficits, including AS, HFA, and NVLD, learn to understand and express empathy and emotions.* Shawnee Mission, KS: Autism Asperger Publishing Company.

Carter, M. A., & Santomauro, J. (2004). *Space travelers: An interactive program for developing social understanding, social competence and social skills for students with Asperger Syndrome, autism and other social cognitive challenges.* Shawnee Mission, KS: Autism Asperger Publishing Company.

Coucouvanis, J. (2005). *Super Skills: A social skills group program for children with Asperger Syndrome, high-functioning autism and related challenges.* Shawnee Mission, KS: Autism Asperger Publishing Company.

Dunn, M. A. (2005). *SOS: Social skills in our schools: A social skills program for children with pervasive developmental disorders, including high-functioning autism, and Asperger Syndrome, and their typical peers.* Shawnee Mission, KS: Autism Asperger Publishing Company.

Fuge, G., & Berry, R. (2004). *Pathways to play! Combining sensory integration and integrated play groups – Theme-based activities for children with autism spectrum and other sensory-processing disorders.* Shawnee Mission, KS: Autism Asperger Publishing Company.

Gutstein, S. E. (2000). *Solving the relationship puzzle. A new developmental program that opens the door to lifelong social and emotional growth.* Ft. Worth, TX: Future Horizons Inc.

Gutstein, S. E., & Sheely, R. K. (2002). *Relationship development intervention with young children. Social and emotional development activities for Asperger's Syndrome, autism, PDD and NLD.* London: Jessica Kingsley Publishers Ltd.

Murdock, L., & Khalsa, G. S. (2003). *Joining In! A program for teaching social skills.* Shawnee Mission, KS: Autism Asperger Publishing Company.

Wolfberg, P. J. (2003). *Peer play and the autism spectrum: The art of guiding children's socialization and imagination.* Shawnee Mission, KS: Autism Asperger Publishing Company.

Appendix

Reward Cards

Here are three types of reward cards to choose from depending on what behavior you are rewarding and the child's area of interest (trains, lizards, and horses).

I am a great listener	I speak politely
I know who to share my space with	I know which voice to use
I am wonderful at waiting	I can listen AND do
I'm learning about emotions	I am a fantastic friend
I know what to do when I get angry	I am great at _____

Bareket, R. *Playing It Right!* 2006. Shawnee Mission, KS: Autism Asperger Publishing Company; www.asperger.net

Reward Cards (cont.)

I am a great listener	**I speak politely**
I know who to share my space with	**I know which voice to use**
I am wonderful at waiting	**I can listen AND do**
I'm learning about emotions	**I am a fantastic friend**
I know what to do when I get angry	**I am great at _____**

Reward Cards (cont.)

I am a great listener	I speak politely

I know who to share my space with	I know which voice to use

I am wonderful at waiting	I can listen AND do

I'm learning about emotions	I am a fantastic friend

I know what to do when I get angry	I am great at _____

 Bareket, R. *Playing It Right!* 2006. Shawnee Mission, KS: Autism Asperger Publishing Company; www.asperger.net

Schedules

Make schedules with the child from the following templates. Keep the schedules visible by hanging them on the classroom wall or refrigerator door for the child to see.

✔ **Materials**
- colored pens, pencils and crayons
- glue
- photos
- old magazines
- your own drawings (stick figures are O.K.)
- pamphlets from activities like train rides, sports, holidays
- copies of pages 60 and 61

To provide the child with his own copy, photocopy all schedules smaller and cover them in plastic so the child can keep them in a pocket, backpack, or pencil case.

The following are just samples of the many types of schedules that may be used.

My Weekly Schedule

The following schedule contains suggestions that you can adjust around your family or school routine.

	Monday	Tuesday	Wednesday	Thursday	Friday
Morning	Breakfast	Breakfast	Breakfast	Breakfast	Breakfast
Afternoon	Lunch	Lunch	Lunch	Lunch	Lunch
Evening	Dinner	Dinner	Dinner	Dinner	Dinner
	Bath	Bath	Bath	Bath	Bath
	Bed	Bed	Bed	Bed	Bed

Bareket, R. *Playing It Right!* 2006. Shawnee Mission, KS: Autism Asperger Publishing Company; www.asperger.net

Pictures and Labels to Cut out and Glue on the Schedule

School	Playdate
TV/DVD	**Park**
Games	**Computer**
Arts and Crafts	**Outside Play**
Rest	**Music**
Dancing	**At Home**

✔ The schedule and activities may be laminated before being cut out. You can attach the activities using Blu Tack™ or similar reusable adhesive. This gives you the flexibility to change activities day to day or week to week. (Illustrations can be pictures cut out from magazines, be drawn freehand or pasted in from software programs such as Boardmaker.)

My Vacation

Draw a picture of something you would like to do during your vacation.

My Vacation Schedule

Month: _____

Monday	Tuesday	Wednesday	Thursday	Friday	Saturday	Sunday

Help the child as needed to add the dates, and then color in school/kindergarten weeks and vacation days in different colors. This will highlight when the vacation is.

 Bareket, R. *Playing It Right!* 2006. Shawnee Mission, KS: Autism Asperger Publishing Company; www.asperger.net

My Vacation

	Day: _____
	Date: _____
Morning	**Breakfast**
Afternoon	**Lunch**
Evening	**Dinner**
	Bath
	Bed

Pictures and Labels to Cut out and Glue on the Schedule

Park		Games	
Arts and Crafts		Outside Play	
Ride Bike		Rest	
Visit Family		Computer	
Playdate		TV/DVD	
Plane Trip		Train Ride	
Swimming		Museum	
Movie		Zoo	

✔ If you are going away, use brochures from your trip to cut out and glue on your daily planner or timetable.

Bareket, R. *Playing It Right!* 2006. Shawnee Mission, KS: Autism Asperger Publishing Company; www.asperger.net

Choice Board

Even during an otherwise well-structured school day, choice boards can be useful for less structured times like lunch, recess – even play. Offering children appropriate choices gives them a sense of control over their lives and can help reduce the occurrence of acting-out behaviors and meltdowns. Combined with schedules, it provides some structure to the child's day – a much-needed security for children on the autism spectrum.

✔ **Materials**
- one large and one small plain wooden board
- Velcro dots
- camera to make choice cards

Hang both boards on the wall. Photograph a range of activities children do in school and at home, depending on where the choice board will be used. Laminate the photos to make cards and attach the Velcro dots both to the cards and the boards. Stick all the cards on the choice board. Help the child choose a sequence of activities that he will do and put them on his own small sequence board.

✔ You can build in flexibility by using a symbol (✪) to represent an activity that you haven't planned yet.

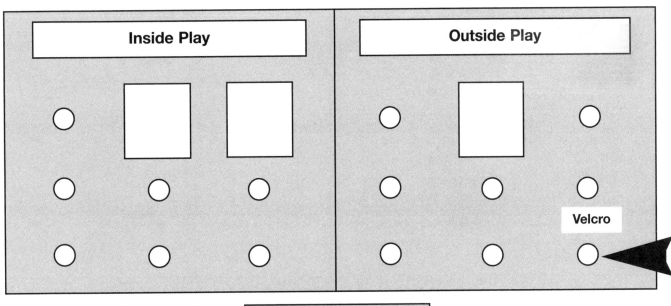

Ideas for Choice Cards

Inside Play		Outside Play	
Blocks		Ball	
Arts and Crafts		Sandbox	
Music		Play Equipment	
Puppets		Play House	
Computer		Tricycle	

Worksheet Templates

Social Skills Checklist

Social Issue The child:	Yes (X)	Section	Page
Has limited concept of family relationships		**Relationships**	4
Has poor eye contact		**Learning to Listen**	6,7
Is unable to stay still while listening		**Learning to Listen**	8
Fails to reply when spoken to		**Learning to Listen**	8
Tends to invade others' body space		**My Special Space**	11
Squeezes/hugs too tightly		**My Special Space**	11
Finds it difficult to discern when and with whom to share body space		**My Special Space**	12
Has difficulty waiting		**Waiting**	15
Is unable to read others' emotion		**Learning About Emotions**	19
Demonstrates anger out of proportion to a given situation		**Dealing with Anger**	28
Is unable to control anger		**Dealing with Anger**	31
Uses impolite and inappropriate language		**Speaking Politely**	34
Uses inappropriately loud voice with no control of dynamics		**Using Our Voices**	36
Is unable to discern emotion in voice		**Using Our Voices**	40
Uses wrong emotion in voice		**Using Our Voices**	40
Demonstrates oppositional behavior (no cooperation)		**Cooperation**	41
Is unable to understand the perspective of others		**Cooperation/Friendship**	41 46-50
Has difficulty understanding the dynamics of play		**Friendship**	46
Has difficulty discerning who friends are		**Friendship**	45, 50
Becomes anxious from not knowing "what will happen next" or during unstructured times		**Schedules to Relieve Anxiety**	59

 Bareket, R. *Playing It Right!* 2006. Shawnee Mission, KS: Autism Asperger Publishing Company; www.asperger.net

My Family Tree

grandparent	grandparent	grandparent	grandparent	grandparent
aunt	aunt	aunt	aunt	aunt
uncle	uncle	uncle	uncle	uncle
brother	brother	brother	brother	brother
sister	sister	sister	sister	sister
cousin	cousin	cousin	cousin	cousin

My Family Tree

Me!

Mom

Dad

Bareket, R. *Playing It Right!* 2006. Shawnee Mission, KS: Autism Asperger Publishing Company; www.asperger.net

Poster – Good Listening

1. Look at the Person

2. Don't Bump Words

3. Keep Still

4. Reply

Who Can I Share My Space With?

With Family, and Sometimes With Teachers and Friends:

Not When We Are Playing or Working:

Never With Strangers:

 Bareket, R. *Playing It Right!* 2006. Shawnee Mission, KS: Autism Asperger Publishing Company; www.asperger.net

Pictures and Labels to Cut out and Glue on the Poster

Family	Friends or Teachers	Strangers
I hug my family!	We don't share our space with friends when they are busy!	
I love to hug my sister.	Sometimes we share our space with friends.	
	Sometimes I need to hug my teacher. (preschool)	
	We don't share space when we are busy in class.	
	I don't share my space during line-up.	

Bareket, R. *Playing It Right!* 2006. Shawnee Mission, KS: Autism Asperger Publishing Company; www.asperger.net

When Do I Need to Wait?

Picture of Child

Picture of Me Waiting When ...

Bareket, R. *Playing It Right!* 2006. Shawnee Mission, KS: Autism Asperger Publishing Company; www.asperger.net

Pictures and Labels to Cut out and Glue on the Poster
I Need to Wait When …

Someone is on the phone.	People are talking.	Dad's cooking.	Mom's feeding the baby.
Mom's bathing the baby.	The teacher is busy.	Someone's watching TV.	My friends are in the middle of playing a game.

Pictures and Labels to Cut out and Glue on the "Wait Card"

Say "Excuse Me."

Take a deep breath.

Count to 10.

12345678910

Don't bump words.

Stay out of people's space.

Go and play.

 Bareket, R. *Playing It Right!* 2006. Shawnee Mission, KS: Autism Asperger Publishing Company; www.asperger.net

Identifying Emotions

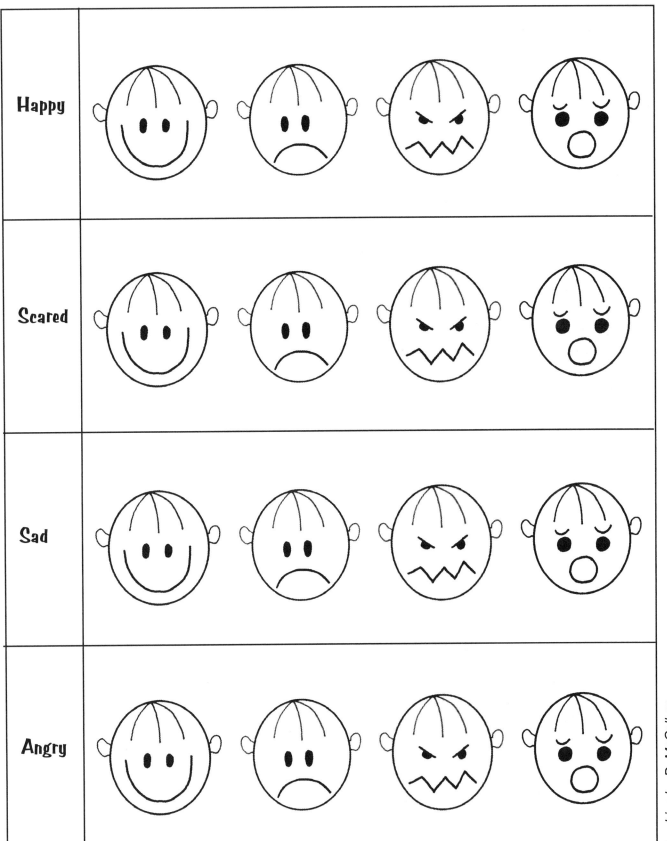

Graphics by D. McCallum

Emotions "Snap" and "Memory"

Happy	Happy	Sad
Happy	Sad	Sad
Happy	Sad	Angry
Angry	Scared	Scared

Bareket, R. *Playing It Right!* 2006. Shawnee Mission, KS: Autism Asperger Publishing Company; www.asperger.net

Emotions "Snap" and "Memory" (cont.)

Angry	Scared	Surprised
Angry	Scared	Surprised
Surprised	Surprised	

Concepts and graphics by D. McCallum

Practice in the Mirror

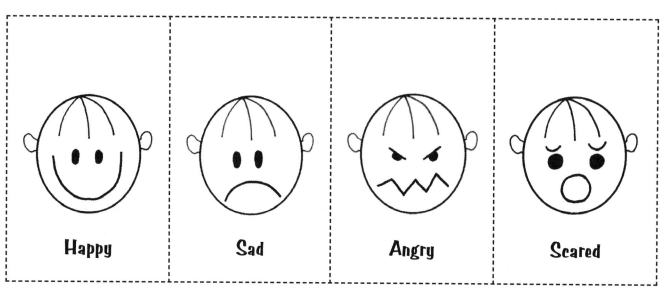

| Happy | Sad | Angry | Scared |

Graphics by D. McCallum

 Bareket, R. *Playing It Right!* 2006. Shawnee Mission, KS: Autism Asperger Publishing Company; www.asperger.net

Spot the Emotion

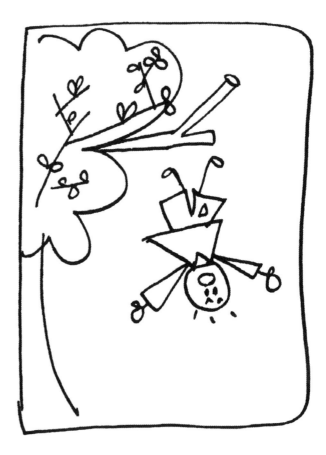

The child feels (circle):

Happy   Sad   Angry   Scared

Happy   Sad   Angry   Scared

Why? _____

_____

_____

Why? _____

_____

_____

Spot the Emotion

The child feels (circle):

Happy   Sad   Angry   Scared   Happy   Sad   Angry   Scared

Why? _____   Why? _____

_____   _____

_____   _____

 Bareket, R. *Playing It Right!* 2006. Shawnee Mission, KS: Autism Asperger Publishing Company; www.asperger.net

Spot the Emotion

The child feels (circle):

Happy   Sad   Angry   Scared

Why? _____

_____

_____

Happy   Sad   Angry   Scared

Why? _____

_____

_____

Spot the Emotion

The child feels (circle):

Happy   Sad   Angry   Scared   Happy   Sad   Angry   Scared

Why? _____   Why? _____

_____   _____

_____   _____

Spot the Emotion

The child feels (circle):

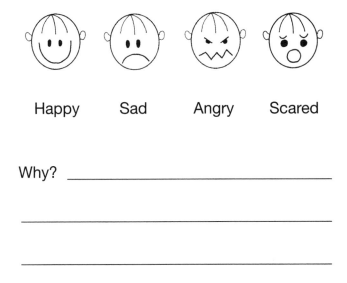

Happy   Sad   Angry   Scared

Why? _____

_____

_____

Grouchometer

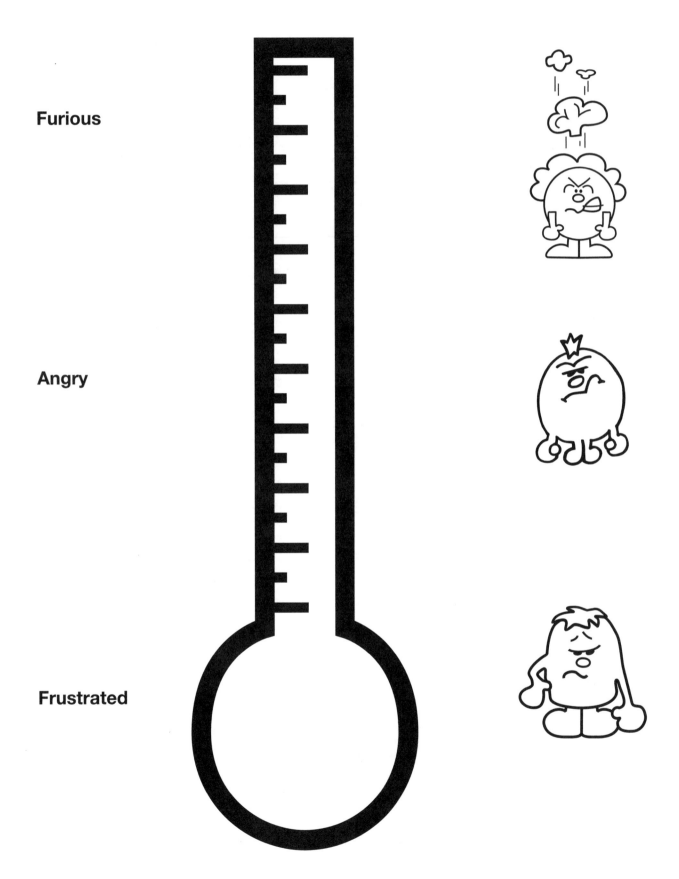

Furious

Angry

Frustrated

Bareket, R. *Playing It RIght!* 2006. Shawnee Mission, KS: Autism Asperger Publishing Company; www.asperger.net

How Angry Am I?	Draw a Circle Around the Matching Level of Anger
Putting together a difficult puzzle	Frustrated Angry Furious
Waiting	Frustrated Angry Furious
Losing my favorite toy	Frustrated Angry Furious

How Angry Am I?	Draw a Circle Around the Matching Level of Anger
Falling over	**Frustrated** **Angry** **Furious**
Someone hits me	**Frustrated** **Angry** **Furious**
Computer problem	**Frustrated** **Angry** **Furious**

 Bareket, R. *Playing It Right!* 2006. Shawnee Mission, KS: Autism Asperger Publishing Company; www.asperger.net

Anger Card

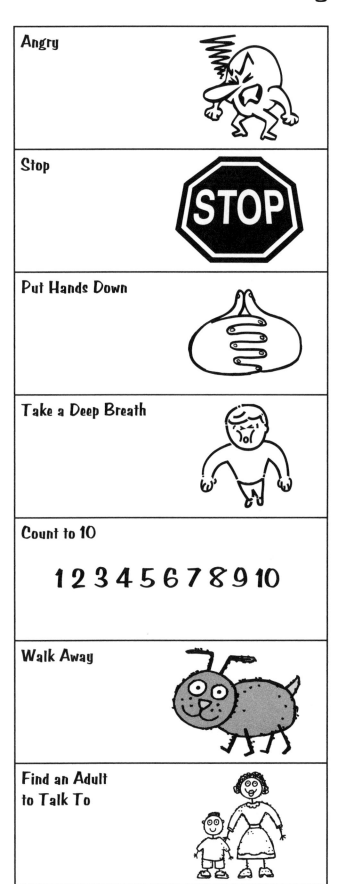

Angry	
Stop	
Put Hands Down	
Take a Deep Breath	
Count to 10	1 2 3 4 5 6 7 8 9 10
Walk Away	
Find an Adult to Talk To	

Calming Activity Cards

Play on the computer.		**Draw a picture about how you are feeling.**	
Play a quiet game such as a puzzle.		**Go for a walk.**	
Go for a run.		**Take a rest.**	
Write a story about how you are feeling.		**Listen to a story tape.**	
Play with your stress ball.		**Visit another teacher or friend.**	

The Trash Program

Better!	I am upset with you.		
Feed It to the Trash Monster!			
Not Nice!	I hate you!		

Practice Using Your Voice

 Bareket, R. *Playing It Right!* 2006. Shawnee Mission, KS: Autism Asperger Publishing Company; www.asperger.net

Which Voice Do I Use?

Place	Voice		
In the park	Soft Voice	Medium Voice	Loud Voice
At the library	Soft Voice	Medium Voice	Loud Voice
In the classroom	Soft Voice	Medium Voice	Loud Voice
At home	Soft Voice	Medium Voice	Loud Voice
At the zoo	Soft Voice	Medium Voice	Loud Voice
In a shop	Soft Voice	Medium Voice	Loud Voice

Which Voice Do I Use?

Place	Voice		
In the street	Soft Voice	Medium Voice	Loud Voice
At the mall	Soft Voice	Medium Voice	Loud Voice
At someone's house	Soft Voice	Medium Voice	Loud Voice
In a hospital	Soft Voice	Medium Voice	Loud Voice
At the movies	Soft Voice	Medium Voice	Loud Voice
In the car	Soft Voice	Medium Voice	Loud Voice
On a bus or train	Soft Voice	Medium Voice	Loud Voice

Listen and Do

Mom and Dad Do Things for Me ...

Photo of
child

So I Will Listen AND Do Things for Them.

Listen and Do

My Teachers Do Things for Me ...

So I Will Listen AND Do Things for Them.

Photo of child

 Bareket, R. *Playing It Right!* 2006. Shawnee Mission, KS: Autism Asperger Publishing Company; www.asperger.net

Listen and Do

Things Mom and Dad Do for Me	Things I Can Do for Mom and Dad	Things My Teachers Do for Me	Things I Can Do for My Teachers
Play with me	Brush my teeth when asked to	Hug me when I'm sad (preschool)	Sit on the mat and listen
Read to me	Go to bed	Help me with painting and drawing	Use my quiet voice inside
Take me to the zoo	Get in the bath or shower when asked to	Teach me games	Eat lunch when asked to
Take me to the beach	Eat breakfast when served	Read to me	Do my work
Make yummy food	Get dressed when it's time	Take me on a field trip	Line up quietly
Give me hugs and kisses	Feed the dog	Help me finish my work	Be good to other kids

Friends Do Things for Each Other

Things My Friends Do for Me

Things I Can Do for My Friends

Photo of
child

    Bareket, R. *Playing It RIght!* 2006. Shawnee Mission, KS: Autism Asperger Publishing Company; www.asperger.net

Friends Do Things for Each Other

Things My Friends Do for Me	Things I Can Do for My Friends
Listen to me	**Listen to them**
Talk about what I like	**Talk about what they like**
Play what I like	**Play what they like**
Teach me games	**Use my happy voice**
Take turns	**Take turns**

Friends Do Things for Each Other

Things My Friends Do for Me	Things I Can Do for My Friends
Not bump words with me	Don't bump words with them
Use a medium voice, not a loud voice	Use a medium voice, not a loud voice
Stay out of my space	Stay out of their space
Help me when I am stuck	Help them when they are stuck
Be happy when I win	Be happy when they win
Don't tease me	Don't tease them

 Bareket, R. *Playing It Right!* 2006. Shawnee Mission, KS: Autism Asperger Publishing Company; www.asperger.net

Who Are My Good Friends?

My Friends	What I Like About Them

Other Titles from AAPC on Social Skills and Young Children

Peer Play and the Autism Spectrum:
The Art of Guiding Children's Socialization and Imagination

Pamela J. Wolfberg

Pathways to Play!
Combining Sensory Integration and Integrated Play Groups

Glenda Fuge and Rebecca Berry

Let's Talk Emotions: Helping Children with Social Cognitive Deficits,
Including AS, HFA, and NVLD, Learn to Understand and Express
Empathy and Emotions

Teresa A. Cardon

Learn to Move, Move to Learn:
Sensorimotor Early Childhood Activity Themes

Jenny Clark Brack

Joining In! A Program for Teaching Social Skills

Linda Murdock and Guru Shabad Khalsa

When My Autism Gets Too Big!
A Relaxation Book for Children with Autism Spectrum Disorders

Kari Dunn Buron; foreword by Brenda Smith Myles

To order: Call 913-897-1004 or visit www.asperger.net

Autism Asperger Publishing Co.
P.O. Box 23173
Shawnee Mission, Kansas 66283-0173
www.asperger.net